MISSION TO MARS

THE VIKING MISSIONS TO MARS

John Hamilton

AB&DO
Daughters Publishing

Visit us at
www.abdopub.com

Published by Abdo Publishing Company, 4940 Viking Drive, Edina, Minnesota 55435.
Copyright ©1998 by Abdo Consulting Group, Inc. International copyrights reserved in all countries. No part of this book may be reproduced in any form without written permission from the publisher.

Interior Graphic Design: John Hamilton
Cover Design: MacLean & Tuminelly
Contributing Editor: Alan Gergen

Cover photo: NASA/JPL
Interior photos: NASA/JPL

Sources: Berman, Louis, & Evans, J.C. *Exploring The Cosmos (2nd ed.).* Boston: Little, Brown and Company, 1977; Caidin, Martin & Barbree, Jay. *Destination Mars.* New York: Penguin Studio, 1997; Chaikin, Andrew. *Hard Landings.* Air & Space, July, 1997, pp. 48-55; Gore, Rick. *Sifting for Life in the Sands of Mars.* National Geographic, January 1977, pp. 9-28; Sagen, Carl. *Cosmos.* New York: Random House, 1980; Sheehan, William. *The Planet Mars: A History of Observation and Discovery.* University of Arizona Press, 1996; *Viking Fact Sheet.* Jet Propulsion Laboratory and NASA's National Space Science Data Center web site, 1997; Vogt, Gregory. *Viking and the Mars Landing.* Brookfield, CT: Millbrook Press, 1991.

Library of Congress Cataloging–in–Publication Data

Hamilton, John, 1959-
    The Viking missions to Mars / John Hamilton
        p. cm. — (Mission to Mars)
    Includes index.
    Summary: Discusses the United States space program Viking and its missions to Mars.
    ISBN 1-56239-829-6
    1. Viking Mars Program (U.S.) 2. Space flight to Mars—Juvenile literature. 3. Mars (Planet)—Exploration—Juvenile literature. 4. Mars probes—Juvenile literature. [1. Mars (Planet)—Exploration. 2. Viking Mars Program. 3. Space flight to Mars.] I. Title. II. Series: Hamilton, John, 1959- Mission to Mars.
TL789.8.U6V525   1998
629.43' 543—dc21   97-34679
                                       CIP
                                       AC

CONTENTS

CHAPTER 1

THE VIKING MISSIONS

In 1976, NASA's twin Viking space probes gave us the most complete view yet of Mars, the mysterious Red Planet. The missions gave us answers about the nature and history of Mars. We now know that it is a cold, forbidding place, with reddish volcanic soil lying under a thin, dry carbon dioxide atmosphere. We're nearly certain, thanks to Viking's legacy, that water once flowed freely over the Martian surface. Evidence of ancient river beds and vast floods abound.

Each Viking spacecraft consisted of an orbiter and a lander. Together, the two orbiters took over 52,000 photographs of Mars, mapping nearly 100 percent of the

The first black-and-white photo of Mars transmitted by *Viking 1*. One of the lander's footpads rests in the foreground.

surface. The landers took a combined 4,500 images of their rocky landing sites, and took more than three million weather measurements.

Most people will probably remember the Viking missions for their search for signs of life on Mars. Each lander was equipped with a robotic arm that scooped up soil samples, then analyzed the specimens in miniature biology labs. Although no life was officially detected, the results were inconclusive. Most of the elements needed for life were found on Mars. Perhaps life exists in some form that we haven't yet detected. Many questions remain unanswered.

An image of Mars as seen by the *Viking 1* orbiter.

Chapter 2

Unanswered Questions

In 1972, the *Mariner 9* space probe began a year-long investigation of Mars. The 1,245-pound (565-kilogram) probe was the first spacecraft to orbit another planet. At the closest approach in its elliptical orbit, *Mariner 9* came within 868 miles (1,388 km) of Mars. This fact, coupled with an advanced photo system (for its time), allowed *Mariner 9* to map 100 percent of Mars' surface after returning 7,329 images.

The portrait of Mars that was revealed astonished NASA scientists. Instead of the "dead" crater-filled planet they were expecting, Mars (especially the Northern Hemisphere) was very interesting indeed. Huge volcanoes rose up from the northern plains, towering higher than anything ever before seen. (Olympus Mons is the tallest mountain in the solar system, climbing 16 miles (25 km) high. It is nearly 373 miles (600 km) wide at its base, about the same size as the state of Arizona.)

The *Mariner 9* spacecraft.

Mariner 9 also revealed a gigantic rift system stretching across almost one fourth of Mars' surface. Vallis Marineris is nearly 3,000 miles (4,827 km) long and up to 15.5 miles (25 km) wide. In some spots, Vallis Marineris is nearly 4.5 miles (7 km) deep, over four times deeper than Earth's Grand Canyon!

But *Mariner 9*'s most important discovery was the hint of water on Mars' surface. The probe's photos clearly showed ancient, dry riverbeds that flowed with liquid long, long ago. Also, many scientists were beginning to think that Mars' north polar cap was not composed entirely of frozen carbon dioxide (dry ice) as first thought, but probably contained frozen water.

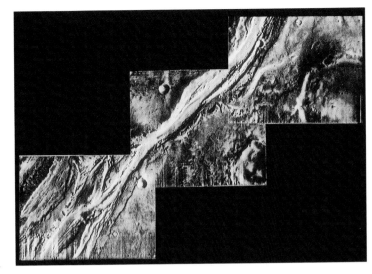

Evidence of water sometime in Mars' distant past is revealed by this image of an ancient riverbed.

The possibility of water on Mars was a very exciting idea. Water is one of the key ingredients of carbon-based life forms like the kind that thrive on Earth. Since it now seemed likely that Mars once held vast quantities of water, perhaps life evolved there as well. And if water was still on Mars, either locked in the polar cap, or maybe in great sheets of permafrost just under the surface, perhaps life still flourished on the Red Planet.

But there was no way to tell for sure from an orbiting space platform like *Mariner 9*. We had to do science experiments on the surface of Mars itself, and to do that we needed to build a new spacecraft that could land safely on the planet. And so, even as *Mariner 9* continued to map Mars, NASA went hard to work on the next generation of Mars probes. It would be one of the last products of NASA's "golden era" of seemingly unlimited manpower and resources. The probe's name was Viking, and it would soon show us a new face of an alien world.

CHAPTER 3

THE TROUBLE WITH LANDERS

The task of landing a probe on an alien planet wasn't exactly a new idea. Both the United States and the Soviet Union had attempted the feat several times before, with varying degrees of success. On December 15, 1970, with the *Venera 7* probe, the Soviets were the first to successfully land a spacecraft on another planet, Venus. This was followed by a string of successful landings in the Venera series. Earlier, during the late 1950s, the United States and Soviet Union competed to land a probe on Earth's moon. The Soviets' *Luna 9* returned the first photographs from the surface on February 4, 1966. The United States tried with its Ranger probes, and then with the Surveyor series. On June 1, 1966, the *Surveyor 1* spacecraft achieved the first American soft landing on the lunar surface, touching down softly in the Ocean of Storms.

One of the toughest hurdles in designing a spacecraft to land on another world is the problem of direct control. When *Apollo 11* ran into trouble during its descent to the moon, human astronauts

Surveyor 1, the first U.S. spacecraft to land softly on the moon.

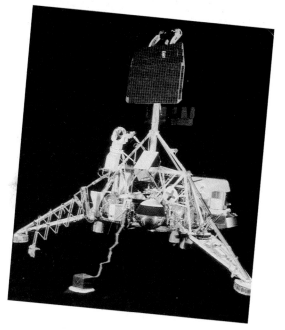

took over control to steer the lander away from a dangerous field of boulders. But interplanetary distances are vast. At its closest approach, Mars is 34 million miles (55 million km) from Earth. The two planets would be even farther apart when the Viking probes were scheduled to land. Even traveling at the speed of light, signals from Viking would still take about 19 minutes to reach Earth. If Viking encountered trouble, the crisis would be over long before NASA could do anything about it. Because of this, Viking had to be self-sufficient and carry out its landing mission without ground control.

Another big problem in designing a remote lander is speed. With no atmosphere in deep space to slow it down, a spacecraft travels incredibly fast. It's a very difficult task to slow a lander down to keep it from exploding on the surface. With the Surveyor missions to the moon, a system of retrorockets, controlled by radar measuring speed and distance from the surface, were fired to slow the probes' descent. At touchdown, *Surveyor 1* was traveling about 10 miles (16 km) per hour, slow enough for its instruments to survive the impact.

The Viking probe would use retrorockets as well, but also had another way to slow its descent—the Martian atmosphere. Even though the air on Mars is very thin, Viking could still use a technique called "aerobraking," which uses the friction caused by going through an atmosphere at high speed to slow down. This generates a lot of heat, though, so the lander would have to be protected with a heatshield. After aerobraking, the probe would make use of the Martian atmosphere again by using a parachute. Retrorockets would slow it down on its final descent.

Many scientists at NASA weren't sure that the Viking program would work. The risk of a crash was very great. The Soviet Union had tried before in 1971 with its *Mars 2* and *Mars 3* landers. Both were unsuccessful, although *Mars 3* did send back a brief television signal from the Martian surface before contact was lost forever. Would the Americans have more luck than their Soviet rivals? The Viking probes would have to be very well designed to succeed.

An artist's rendering of a Viking lander touching down on the surface of Mars.

CHAPTER 4

• • • • • • • • • • • • • •

THE SPACECRAFT

In the early 1970s, NASA decided that the Viking missions to Mars would consist of two identical spacecraft, called *Viking 1* and *Viking 2*. Each ship would include a lander to conduct experiments on the Martian surface, plus an orbiter, which would take high-resolution color images of the Red Planet. It would be the most complex mission ever to explore Mars.

The Viking orbiters were much bigger than the previous Mariner spacecraft, each weighing 5,115 pounds (2,320 kg). One of the reasons the Vikings were so much heavier was because they needed to carry more fuel, which would be used to slow down the spacecraft and their attached landers when they reached Mars orbit.

The main part of the Viking orbiters were box-like structures about 8 feet (2.4 meters) across. This section contained the photo imagers, radio antennas, and other scientific equipment. Mounted on top of the spacecraft was the lander, nestled safely inside a pod shaped like a flattened egg. This was called the "aeroshell." The lander would piggyback all the way to Mars until it reached orbit, where it would separate and drop to the Martian surface.

The Viking orbiter/ lander. The lander is safely encased inside the aeroshell on top of the orbiter.

The orbiter got its power from four projecting panels made of thousands of solar cells that converted sunlight to electricity. With the solar panels in place, each spacecraft measured about 32 feet (9.7 meters) across.

To guide the orbiters on their way to Mars, two sensors kept track of the position of the sun and the star Canopus. If these two markers were in the proper position, then the probes were pointed in the right direction. If a mid-course correction was needed, the spacecraft could be re-aimed by firing small nitrogen gas jets mounted on the tips of the solar panels.

The Viking landers, each about the size of a Jeep, were marvels of engineering for their time. Made of aluminum and titanium alloys, the landers were fitted with an array of scientific instruments, communications gear, cameras, plus landing rockets mounted underneath. Miniature biological laboratories were included to search for microscopic Martian life. Twin onboard computers held 18,000 words of memory in a case about the size of a small duffle bag, which was an amazing feat of computer science engineering for the mid 1970s. (Today, home computers can include several megabytes of memory for less than $100.) Also on board were instruments to measure Martian weather, plus a seismometer to detect possible Mars-quakes.

The four Viking spacecraft (two landers and two orbiters) cost about $930 million dollars ($3 billion in today's dollars). Of that cost, nearly one fourth was spent in a crucial part of getting the landers ready for their mission—sterilization. Searching for Martian lifeforms was one of the main goals of the Viking project. The entire mission would be ruined if the landers detected

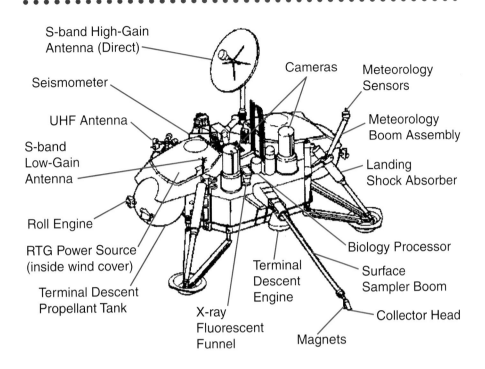

S-band High-Gain
Antenna (Direct)

Seismometer

UHF Antenna

S-band
Low-Gain
Antenna

Roll Engine

RTG Power Source
(inside wind cover)

Terminal Descent
Propellant Tank

X-ray
Fluorescent
Funnel

Cameras

Meteorology
Sensors

Meteorology
Boom Assembly

Landing
Shock Absorber

Biology Processor

Surface
Sampler Boom

Collector Head

Terminal
Descent
Engine

Magnets

Earth-born bacteria that mistakenly hitchhiked a ride to Mars. To prevent this, the Vikings were painstakingly sterilized by baking each lander at 234 degrees Fahrenheit (112 degrees Celsius) for 40 hours. This procedure was very hard on the on-board electronics, and it took over two years of testing before everything was safeguarded enough to undergo the actual sterilization procedure. After the landers were sterilized, they were encased in an outer "bioshell" to keep them germ free.

Many scientists thought this costly sterilization procedure was a waste of time and money. Privately, they believed that the landers had almost no chance of surviving the descent to Mars anyway. So many things could go wrong: the Vikings could land in a crater and tip over, or they could hit a large rock or boulder. High winds might make the landers crash. The retrorockets might malfunction, or the parachutes might fail.

A diagram showing the various parts of a Viking lander.

Two years earlier, the Soviet Union had tried again to land a craft on Mars. But *Mars 7* completely missed the planet by 800 miles (1,280 km) because of a guidance system failure. *Mars 6* crashed on the surface. The stage was set for the Americans.

On August 20, 1975, a powerful Titan III Centaur rocket blasted off from Cape Canaveral in Florida. The launch went very smoothly, starting the *Viking 1* space probe on its year-long journey to Mars. On September 9, 1975, less than three weeks later, *Viking 2* followed its twin toward the Red Planet.

The *Viking 1* spacecraft lifts off from its launchpad on Cape Canaveral.

CHAPTER 5

TOUCHDOWN

The journey took nearly one year through 440 million miles (704 million km) of deep space, but on June 19, 1976, *Viking 1* finally arrived in orbit around Mars. It approached the planet at 5,500 miles (8,800 km) per hour relative to Mars. Retrorockets in the orbiter fired as planned, and soon the spacecraft settled into an elliptical (egg-shaped) orbit.

Above: An artist's rendering of a Viking lander separating from its orbiter and touching down on Mars.

This panoramic image shows the rock-strewn terrain of the *Viking 1* landing site. Viking's meteorology boom assembly can be seen in the center of the photo.

Three days later the orbiter sent the first images back to Earth. The photos were stunning in their detail; nothing that clear had ever before been seen of the Martian surface. But scientists were stunned for another reason—the landing site for *Viking 1* was much rougher than was expected. Boulders and gullies were everywhere, making it likely that the lander would crash.

NASA had originally hoped to land on July 4. But they wisely decided that crashing on Mars wouldn't be a very good way to celebrate Independence Day. By using the orbiter's high-resolution cameras, NASA spent the next several weeks finding a safer site for the lander. They finally found their spot in a part of Mars called Chryse Planitia, which is a smooth basin north of the equator.

On July 20, 1976, (the anniversary of the *Apollo 11* moon landing) the *Viking 1* lander separated from the orbiter. The egglike protective bioshell was discarded. Rockets in the lander fired, breaking its orbit so that it could begin its long, arching fall to the Martian surface.

The lander zoomed into Mars' upper atmosphere, protected by its aeroshell heatshield. The aeroshell was made of an aluminum alloy coated with a cork-like material. Soon the lander hit speeds of 10,000 miles (16,000 km) per hour. At that speed friction soon began building up on the heatshield, even though the atmosphere on Mars is very thin. As planned, the cork-like covering burned away, keeping heat away from the lander inside. From the Martian surface, *Viking 1*'s descent probably looked like a flaming streak across the sky, like a falling meteor. This "aerobraking" through the atmosphere slowed the lander down to just over 500 miles (800 km) per hour.

Four miles (six km) above the surface, a small cannon pushed out a billowing red and white parachute to further slow down the lander's descent. The lander soon slowed to just over 100 miles (160 km) per hour. At about 4,000 feet (1,200 meters), explosive bolts jettisoned what was left of the heatshield. Viking's three landing legs automatically stretched out. The legs were spring-loaded to cushion the impact of landing. After another minute, the parachute detached, and three radar-controlled retro rockets, called vernier engines, ignited under the lander to slow it down even more.

At 8:12 A.M., Eastern Daylight Time, the *Viking 1* lander gently touched down on Mars, impacting the surface at about 4.5 miles per hour (2 meters per second). (You would experience about the same impact as jumping off a tall kitchen stool.)

For 19 maddening minutes, controllers at NASA could only sit and wait as the signal from Viking sped through the vacuum of space toward Earth. Was the lander safe, or did it crash? Then came joy as word raced through mission control: "Touchdown! We have touchdown!"

A scene from the *Viking 1* landing site. "Big Joe" is at far left. To the right is the lander's meteorology boom and sensors. On the ground at far right are trenches made by the lander's surface sampler boom.

Shortly after landing, Viking switched on its cameras. The people of Earth were in awe as images from an alien world reached their eyes. Scientists looking at the pictures thanked their lucky stars: the "smooth" landing site was littered with rocks. One large boulder nearby (later named "Big Joe") was as big as the lander itself. If Viking had veered off just a little bit, it would have hit the boulder and crashed for sure.

Less than seven weeks later, *Viking 2* joined its twin on Mars. There was a brief scare as a power failure caused communications to be lost just after separation with the orbiter. But a backup system worked, and *Viking 2* knew what to do on its own, without ground control help. On September 3, 1976, the lander touched down safely at Mars' Utopia Planitia, about 4,000 miles (6,400 km) west of *Viking 1*.

The first color image sent by the *Viking 1* lander.

CHAPTER 6

· · · · · · · · · · · · · ·

SEARCHING FOR LIFE

Each Viking lander soon began sending high-resolution images back to Earth. The on-board cameras used movable mirrors to scan a narrow vertical scene. The camera rotated slightly, and then scanned another swath. By combining each image, NASA was able to obtain wide, panoramic images of the Martian surface. Most of the images were black and white, but later special filters were used to obtain full-color photos.

The surface of each landing site was strewn with rocks and boulders of various shapes and sizes. In many ways the scene resembled the deserts of the Southwest United States. In between the rocks, an orange-colored dusty, sandy soil covered the ground. It lay in drifts, the product of Martian winds. Later, the landers chemically analyzed the soil: it was like a loosely packed iron-rich clay. It got its color from a chemical reaction called oxidation—in other words, rust.

The Martian sky, unlike the pale blue that was expected, turned out to be a salmon-hued pink. Scientists concluded that small dust particles in the air give Mars its pinkish color.

When *Viking 1*'s first day came to an end, it issued the first weather report from Mars: "Light winds from the east in the late afternoon, changing to light winds from the southwest after midnight. Maximum wind, 15 miles (24 km) per hour. Temperature ranging from –122 degrees Fahrenheit (–86 degrees Celsius) just after dawn to –22 degrees Fahrenheit (–30 degrees Celsius)."

After eight days of taking photos and measuring weather conditions on Mars, scientists were ready to begin the search for life. Some had hoped to see some kind of life in the images—footprints of small animals, perhaps, or moss or lichens growing on nearby rocks. But nothing was ever found. Scientists would have to resort to using Viking's on-board biology labs in their hunt for Martian life.

Viking 1 extends its robotic sampler arm and scoop.

Each Viking lander was equipped with three biology laboratories. A 6-foot (1.8-meter) long robotic arm scooped up soil samples and delivered them to the labs. Several instruments were designed to detect even the slightest evidence of life. For example, on Earth plants "eat" carbon dioxide gas, and this can be measured. Also, certain chemical tests were performed to see if microorganisms were present in the soil samples.

At first, some of the tests came back positive. Newspapers spread the word that life had been discovered on Mars! But the excitement was short-lived. After further study, NASA scientists decided that the strange results of the biology labs were the result of some sort of exotic chemical reaction in the soil itself. No Martians had been discovered yet.

Viking 1's robotic arm scoops up a sample of Martian soil.

Most biologists think that the soil on Mars is too sterile to support life. Water in its liquid form cannot exist on the planet today. The air is too cold and dry. Some water vapor was detected in the atmosphere, and this sometimes settles to the ground as frost, but liquid water has never been observed. Another obstacle to life is the deadly ultraviolet radiation from the sun that bombards the planet's surface.

All hope for finding life on Mars is not gone, however. One of the assumptions that scientists made was that life on Mars would be like life on Earth—carbon based. Carbon molecules form the basic building blocks of all life as we know it. But perhaps life exists on Mars in some other form—silicon based, perhaps—and we simply haven't devised a test to detect it yet.

Viking Project Scientist Dr. Gerald Soffen said, "Scientists finally concluded that we found no evidence of life on Mars. But this doesn't prove there is not life on Mars. It simply says that, in the two distinct places on the planet that we landed, there are probably no living organisms."

What seems more likely, however, is that Mars today is a dead planet, in the sense of life existing on its surface. All the critical elements for life on Earth were found on Mars—carbon, nitrogen, hydrogen, oxygen and phosphorus—except for liquid water. But water once flowed freely early in its history, proving that at one time the planet's atmosphere was thicker and warmer. Perhaps eons ago life thrived on Mars. Some scientists think that the only way to tell for sure is to get a soil sample back to Earth for further study—or send human astronauts to the Red Planet.

Right: A computer-generated image showing a side view of Olympus Mons.

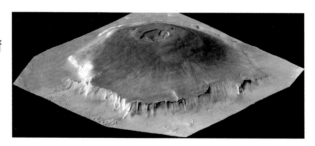

Below: Olympus Mons, as seen by the *Viking 1* orbiter.

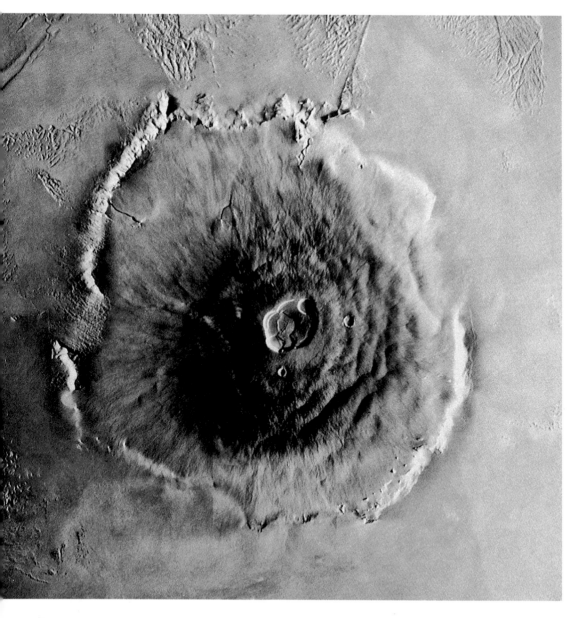

CHAPTER 7

. . . .

OTHER DISCOVERIES

While the landers did their work on the surface of Mars, the Viking orbiters made some startling discoveries of their own. In addition to sending back an astounding 52,000 high-resolution color photographs of the surface, they also made several important findings.

One of the big questions surrounding Mars is: where did all the water go? Ancient riverbeds prove that liquid water once flowed freely across the surface. Where is it today? The Viking orbiters gave two possible explanations.

First, the permanent north polar cap (the part that doesn't melt away during the summer months) is made mostly of *water ice*, not frozen carbon dioxide (dry ice) like scientists first thought.

Secondly, the orbiters discovered that Mars contains thick layers of *permafrost*, frozen water just beneath the surface. It discovered this by providing detailed photos of impact craters. When something hits a planet's surface, such as meteorites, the material that is thrown up around the impact zone (ejecta) is spread out in a predictable way. On Mars, though, many times the craters have

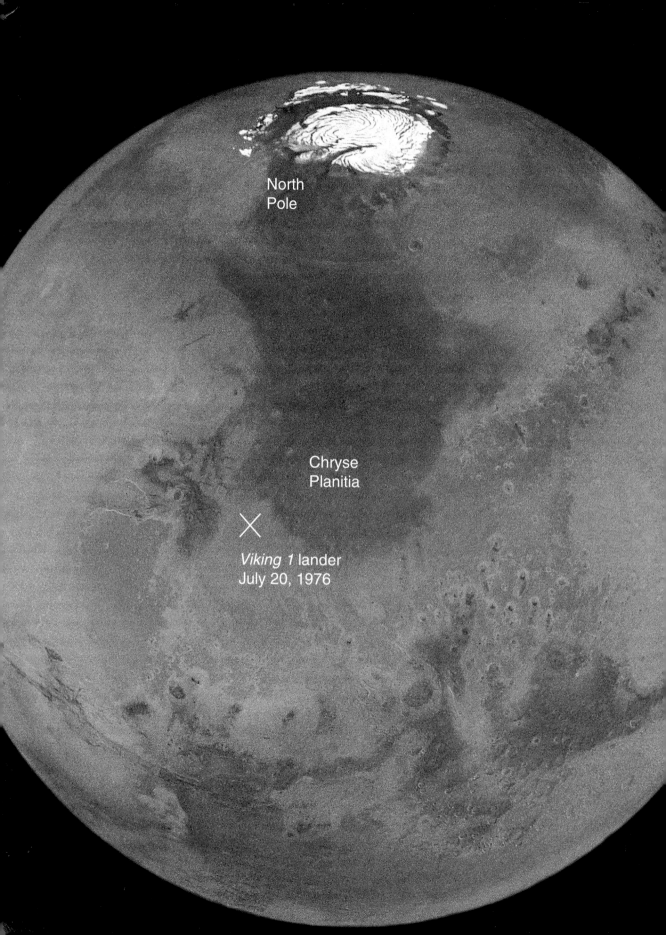

North
Pole

Chryse
Planitia

Viking 1 lander
July 20, 1976

bizarre flow patterns around them. Scientists think that the extreme heat of impact melted permafrost under the surface, turning the ejecta into a kind of sludge, which then flowed and splattered away from the crater.

In addition to studying the surface, the orbiters also trained their cameras on Mars' two moons, Phobos and Deimos. By analyzing the density and physical properties of the moons, NASA scientists think that they are both probably asteroids, caught in Mars' field of gravity millions of years ago.

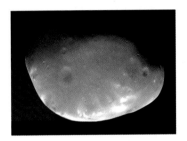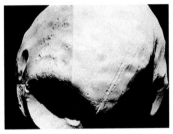

Above: Deimos (left) and Phobos (right), Mars' two moons. Each is probably an asteroid, caught in the planet's gravitational field long ago.

Facing page: A digital photo mosaic made by combining several images from the Viking orbiters. The north polar cap, which is made mostly of water ice, is plainly visible at the top of the photo.

CHAPTER 8

· · · · · · · · · · · · · · ·

THE NEXT STEP

Both Viking missions lasted much longer than planned. Each spacecraft was designed to operate for 90 days after landing, but they went far beyond their mission. Two years after it began orbiting Mars, the *Viking 2* orbiter finally ran out of the fuel it used to keep its solar panels pointed at the sun. With no way to generate electricity, it began drifting away. NASA shut down its systems on July 25, 1978, after 706 orbits.

NASA scientists figured out a way to conserve fuel on the *Viking 1* orbiter. It operated for a total of over four years. Finally, it too ran out of fuel, and was powered down by NASA on August 17, 1980, after 1,489 orbits.

The Viking landers also lasted much longer than expected. The *Viking 2* lander stopped sending signals on April 11, 1980. The *Viking 1* lander ceased functioning on November 11, 1982. Together, they transmitted over 4,500 images of the Martian surface.

Much of what we know about Mars we've learned from the Viking program. In fact, data returned from the probes is still being analyzed. But many, many questions still remain, especially the question of whether life exists, or has ever existed, on Mars. To find answers, we would have to go back someday to that remote, forbidding planet.

Candor Chasma, part of Valles Marineris, Mars' enormous canyon system.

INTERNET SITES

Starchild: A learning center for young astronomers
http://starchild.gsfc.nasa.gov/

This lively site, a service of the Laboratory for High Energy Astrophysics at NASA, is full of information on the solar system, astronauts, and space travel. It has a very good section on Mars covering the main features of the Red Planet, including photos.

Mars Missions
http://mpfwww.jpl.nasa.gov/

This NASA web page provides up-to-the-minute information and photographs on three current space probes: *Mars Pathfinder*, *Mars Global Surveyor*, and *Mars Surveyor 98*.

The Whole Mars Catalog
http://www.reston.com/astro/mars/catalog.html

This is a very extensive site of Mars facts and photos, with many links to other related web sites. Some of the many topics include Mars facts, breaking news from NASA, space probes, and the push to put humans on Mars.

These sites are subject to change. Go to your favorite search engine and type in "Mars" for more sites.

PASS IT ON

Space buffs: educate readers around the country by passing on information you've learned about Mars and space exploration. Share your little-known facts and interesting stories. We want to hear from you!

To get posted on the ABDO & Daughters website, E-mail us at "Science@abdopub.com"

Visit the ABDO & Daughters website at www.abdopub.com

GLOSSARY

· · · · · · · · · · · · · · · · · · ·

asteroids

Small, planetlike objects that revolve around the sun, usually between the orbits of Mars and Jupiter. Their size ranges from one to several hundred miles in diameter. Mars' two moons, Phobos and Deimos, are probably asteroids captured by the planet's gravitational pull millions of years ago.

probe

A probe is an unmanned space vehicle that is sent on missions that are too dangerous, or would take too long, for human astronauts to accomplish. Probes are equipped with many scientific instruments, like cameras and radiation detectors. Information from these instruments is radioed back to ground controllers on Earth.

rocket

A vehicle that moves because of the ejection of gases made by the burning of a self-contained propellant. The propellant is made up of fuel, like liquid hydrogen, and an oxidant like liquid oxygen, which helps the fuel to burn. Sometimes solid explosives are used, like nitroglycerin and nitrocellulose. Solid-fuel rockets are more reliable, but generate less thrust. Some spacecraft, like the United States' Space Shuttle, use a combination of solid and liquid fuel rocket boosters. Rockets were probably invented by the Chinese almost 1,000 years ago, when they stuffed gunpowder into bamboo pipes to make weapons.

solar panel

Many space probes use solar panels, which are large arrays of connected solar cells, to generate electricity. Solar cells are semiconductor devices that convert the energy of sunlight into electric energy. Electricity is needed to power the probe's science experiments, guidance systems, and radios. Some probes, especially those that travel far from the sun to explore the outer planets, rely on internal nuclear power plants to generate electricity. The Cassini probe to Saturn, launched in October of 1997 and due to arrive in 2004, uses a nuclear generator.

solar system

The sun, the nine planets, and other celestial bodies (like asteroids) that orbit the sun. The nine planets are (in order from the sun): Mercury, Venus, Earth, Mars, Jupiter, Saturn, Uranus, Neptune, and Pluto.

star

A large, self-containing ball of gas that is "self luminous," or emits light. Stars come in many sizes, ranging from white dwarfs to red giants. The sun is a medium-sized yellow star. At night, stars are seen as twinkling points of light, which is one way to tell them apart from planets, which do not twinkle.

telescope

A device to detect and observe distant objects by their reflection or emission of various kinds of electromagnetic radiation (like light). Most astronomy research today is conducted with telescopes that detect electromagnetic radiation other than visible light, such as radio or x-ray telescopes.

INDEX